A Touch of His Joy

Other Books in This Series

A Touch of His Freedom
A Touch of His Goodness
A Touch of His Love
A Touch of His Peace
A Touch of His Power
A Touch of His Wisdom

Meditations on God's Abiding Joy

A Touch of His Joy

with Original Photographs by

Charles Stanley

ZONDERVAN™

GRAND RAPIDS, MICHIGAN 49530

ZONDERVAN™

A Touch of His Joy
Copyright © 2001 by Charles F. Stanley

Requests for information should be addressed to:

Zondervan, *Grand Rapids, Michigan 49530*

Library of Congress Cataloging-in-Publication Data

Stanley, Charles F.
    A touch of His joy : meditations of God's abiding joy, with original pho-
tographs by/ Charles Stanley.
       p. cm.
    ISBN 0-310-21493-9
    1. Joy—Religious aspects—Christianity—Meditations   I. Title.
BV4647.J68 S73 2001
242—dc21   2001026580

This edition printed on acid-free paper.

Interior design by Sherri L. Hoffman

Printed in the United States of America

01 02 03 04 05 06 07 /❖ DC/ 10 9 8 7 6 5 4 3 2 1

To Bill Fortney,
One of my favorite photographers,
whose friendship has brought me
a great deal of joy

Contents

	Photographs	9
	Acknowledgments	11
	Introduction	13
1.	A Simple Joy	17
2.	Beyond Bitterness	21
3.	Celebrating Forgiveness	25
4.	Choose Joy	29
5.	Dealing with Anger	33
6.	Delighting in the Lord	37
7.	Difficult People	41
8.	Fresh Encounters with God	45
9.	Fullness of Joy	49
10.	Rejoice!	53
11.	God's Keeping Power	57
12.	God Is Good	61
13.	Great Joy	65
14.	Joy in the Journey	69
15.	Joy Runs Deep	73
16.	Restful Joy	77
17.	Just Do It	81
18.	Let God Choose	85
19.	Man of Joy	89
20.	Many Thanks	93

21.	No Surprise	97
22.	Not So Joyful	101
23.	Pass It Around	105
24.	Sheer Joy	109
25.	Spoiling the Thief	113
26.	The Way of Submission	117
27.	The Joy of the Lord	121
28.	The Source of Joy	125
29.	Truth or Feelings	129
30.	When You're Weary	133
31.	Winning the Battle for Joy	137

Photographs

1.	Early Light, Yellowstone	16
2.	Tetons & Lodge, Wyoming	20
3.	Fire Hole Canyon, Yellowstone	24
4.	Mont Blanc, Aosta, Italy	28
5.	Snowy Falls, Yellowstone	32
6.	Mountain Glacier, Aosta, Italy	36
7.	Mountain & Waterfall, Serrione, Italy	40
8.	Chapel on the Mountain, Serrione, Italy	44
9.	Bent Tree, Aosta, Italy	48
10.	Bristlecone Pine, Utah	52
11.	Rocky Butte, Utah	56
12.	North Window Arch, Arches National Park	60
13.	Bryce Canyon, Utah	64
14.	Old Wagon, Utah	68
15.	Buffalo Rock, Wyoming	72
16.	Grand Tetons, Wyoming	76
17.	Winding Creek, Yellowstone	80
18.	Shane's Cabin, Wyoming	84
19.	Tetons & Valley, Wyoming	88
20.	Mushroom Rocks, Utah	92
21.	Monument Valley, Utah	96
22.	Pueblo Dwellings, Utah	100
23.	Oregon Rock, Utah	104

24.	Chimney Rock, Colorado	108
25.	River Reflections, Wyoming	112
26.	Snowy Creek, Wyoming	116
27.	Elk Crossing, Yellowstone	120
28.	Grand Teton & Pines, Wyoming	124
29.	Snow Covered Fence, Wyoming	128
30.	Frozen Pines, Continental Divide, Idaho	132
31.	Footprints in Snow, Wyoming	136

Acknowledgments

I want to express my appreciation to Bob Schipper, my very able assistant at In Touch, in the preparation of *A Touch of His Joy.*

Introduction

Many Christians are familiar with the prophet Isaiah's description of the Messiah as one who was "a man of sorrows and familiar with sufferings" (Isaiah 53:3). Not so many are acquainted with the writer of Hebrews reference, quoting the psalmist, that Jesus Christ was anointed with the "oil of joy" above everyone else (Hebrews 1:9).

Jesus was—and is—a joyous Savior and he shares his joy with us through the incredible indwelling of the Holy Spirit. The believer in Christ is the only person in the world today who can stake a certified claim to the consistent experience of genuine, undiluted joy.

God's joy runs deep, independent of the comings and goings of our circumstances. We all know how a good day can turn bad, a sweet relationship sour, a promising job disappointing. The wonderful news about Christ's joy is that it does not ride the emotional and happenstance surf of our circumstances.

Rather the solid, consistent joy of God flows strong and consistent in bad times as well as good. The sovereign, loving Spirit of God imparts his joy so that we are sustained and strengthened. Joy that is coupled with the sure knowledge that God knows and God cares allows us to keep our spiritual and moral bearings in any difficulty.

What a tremendous encouragement! We can experience a steady stream of God's empowering joy in any situation. We can celebrate his blessings with thanksgiving and even consider it "pure joy" when we face trials. This is not impractical spiritualizing or oversimplification; it is reckoning on God's sufficiency and superabundant supply for our every need.

An old saint once remarked that joy was the "distinctive hall-mark of the Christian." When the world—our neighborhoods, our workplaces, our schools—are so devoid of true joy and hope, Christians can exhibit the remarkable reality of Christ in us through a life infected by the joy of Jesus.

The great builder and statesmen Nehemiah told the sullen Hebrews that the "joy of the Lord is your strength" (Nehemiah 8:10). I believe this is God's word to us today as we face incredible challenges and strains in a joyless world. God's joy—his presence, power, and love—leads us, keeps us, and enriches us.

May this indescribable joy rise in your heart and soul as you read *A Touch of His Joy* and strengthen you to face test, trial, and temptation with renewed confidence and faith.

A Touch of His Joy

The LORD protects the simplehearted.

PSALM 116:6

A Simple Joy

$\mathcal{L}$ ife can be complicated. There are growing responsibilities for family and work, mounting financial and social pressures, and a seemingly infinite to-do list. These increasing demands often prompt us to seek out ways and means to simplify our lives and reduce the stress by returning to some basic convictions—don't spend more than you make; work hard, but leave time for play; pay attention to details, but don't stay up nights worrying about them.

The same malady occurs in the spiritual domain. We grow older, but not necessarily wiser in our faith. We become busier in our service to the Lord, but not particularly happy. We spend time in the spiritual disciplines, but we do so reluctantly, not cheerfully. We lose the joy and simplicity of childlike faith. The passion and spontaneity of knowing Christ as our "first love" dims.

No formulaic answers exist to recover our joy, but the prophet Micah gives us some realistic guidelines that can help us keep our faith uncluttered.

Instead of approaching and relating to the Lord based on demanding rules (Micah 6:6–7), the prophet summarized what God expects and endorses: "He has showed you, O man, what is good. And what does the LORD require of you? To act justly and to love mercy and to walk humbly with your God" (v. 8).

Pleasing the Lord and enjoying him forever is not complex. God did not design it that way. We throttle out the simple joy he intends by adding too many jots and tittles. Micah's message almost 1,800 years ago is incredibly relevant today.

"Act justly," Micah says. Do the thing you know is right. Don't compromise the truth. Don't develop a belief system founded on rationalization. Just do the right thing as the Spirit and Word of God instruct. Obey the few things you know to do and quit worrying about the rest for right now. Love your family. Give a tithe to the Lord. Don't quarrel; be a peacemaker. Obedience to the truth revealed is the principle. Obedience to God's truth brings freedom, and freedom breeds simplicity, uncluttering our lives from the confusing maze of too many options and choices. The cellist who practices each day is freer to perform in concert than the person who dreams of the stage, but never prepares.

"Love mercy," says Micah. Instead of insisting on your own rights, give them up to the Lord. Put others first, not yourself. Don't treat others as they deserve, but extend mercy as God deals mercifully with you. *Love* mercy, that is, make it a priority in your life. Give God the credit, be gracious to others, and let God take care of your reputation and rewards.

"Walk humbly with your God," Micah encourages. Esteem God and have an accurate view of yourself. Remember that all things good and great come from him. He is the source of all blessings. Acknowledge him in all your ways and keep Christ at the center of all you do.

Think on these things. When the pressure is overwhelming, put these principles into action. It won't be easy, but it sure will keep your faith basic and will make room for a simple joy.

Somehow, I know, Lord, that my life doesn't need to be so complicated. I ask for your quiet confidence to fill my heart and, from that stillness and surety, to direct my steps and order my thoughts. Teach me what is important to you and help me to keep you at the center of all I think and do. When I am distracted and frustrated by the busyness of it all, stop me just for a moment and speak your peace to my soul. Then let me move on in your strength.

Touchstone

Keep your faith simple

and your joy

will prosper.

The plans of the LORD stand firm forever, the
purposes of his heart through all generations.

PSALM 33:11

Beyond Bitterness

How can we deal with heartache without becoming bitter? How do we cope with tragic or unjust incidents in our own lives without succumbing to the toxin of a bitter spirit?

I have always found comfort in the life of Joseph. If ever there was a guy who had plenty of reasons for a foul attitude, it was Joseph. Almost everyone he knew betrayed him. His jealous brothers traded him away to merchants for some fast cash. After he was sold to an Egyptian official, his master's wife falsely accused him of sexual harassment. A servant he befriended in Pharaoh's court quickly forgot his kindness and wisdom after he was released. It wasn't until Joseph was thirty years old, about thirteen years after his brothers' dastardly act, that he was elevated to one of Egypt's highest offices.

Had Joseph sulked and grown resentful in his circumstances—and he certainly had plenty of opportunity—he would have never been ready to assume the lofty position of leadership suddenly offered him by Pharaoh. A bitter person typically becomes isolated, withdrawn, and virtually incapable of positive interaction with others.

I am convinced that the fundamental basis for Joseph's perseverance and deliverance from a bitter spirit was his insight into God's sovereign hand in his difficulties. After an emotional disclosure of his identity to his brothers, Joseph said, "And now, do not be distressed and do not be angry with yourselves for selling me here, because it was to save lives that God sent me ahead of you. . . . So then, it was not you who sent me here, but God" (Genesis 45:5, 8). Later Joseph reemphasized God's providential control of his life as he spoke to his remorseful siblings, "You intended to harm me, but God intended it for good to accomplish what is now being done, the saving of many lives" (Genesis 50:20).

Many people caused Joseph much pain, none of which was just or right. The only way he avoided the spiritual wasteland of a bitter heart was embracing God's control of the events that adversely affected him. Joseph's brothers did sell him into bondage, but not without God's permission and not apart from God's power and knowledge. Behind the scenes, permitting but not causing the grievous events of Joseph's life, was the Lord.

As difficult as it may be to accept, I suggest the sole way to keep your heart cleansed of the poison of bitterness is to see the Lord's hand in all circumstances and believe that he will use the treacherous, cruel acts of others to accomplish his purpose in your life. When you say to the Lord, "My times are in your hands" (Psalm 31:15), you acknowledge God's ultimate sovereignty over your life. Rather than fixating on the problems that have afflicted you, turn to the good hand of the Lord and entrust yourself into his loving care.

See God at work in all things. Firmly believe that he is able to use your tangled and snarled circumstances for your eventual good. Don't deny the hurt or loss, but never lose sight of God's triumphant involvement in all of your affairs.

I thank you, Lord, because I can avoid the strangling grip of a bitter spirit by embracing your sovereign and loving help in encounters and events that prove difficult at best. I praise you because you make it possible to experience your joy in the worst, as well as the best, of times. Your joy is never diminished by my circumstances, and you give it freely to those who put their wholehearted trust in you.

Touchstone

We can give thanks in
everything because God
works all things together
for good.

But we had to celebrate and be glad.

LUKE 15:32

Celebrating Forgiveness

$\mathcal{T}$he scene is festive. A feast is being prepared. Servants scurry about the house, putting together all the details for a lively party. A fresh wardrobe is readied for the main guest and center of attention. Unbridled joy throbs in the heart of the host.

You know the story of the prodigal son, the young man who wasted money and lived raucously. He returned to his father's home broke and broken. "Father, I have sinned against heaven and against you. I am no longer worthy to be called your son" (Luke 15:21). The father didn't scold or berate; rather, he called for a celebration.

The story is the narrative of God's own forgiveness for each of his children. It echoes the great theme of the gospel—forgiveness of sin, the work that Christ accomplished on the cross for men and women who squander their lives in self-centered living. Wherever there is forgiveness, there is much joy. Wherever there is unforgiveness, there is anger and alienation.

Christians should be the happiest people on earth, because the Father in heaven has forgiven them of their sins. The Judge of people's souls has, through the justice of the cross, released us from the guilt of our sins and its severe penalty—eternal death. We don't have to strive or beg to receive God's forgiveness; we already have it through the sacrificial death of Jesus Christ. The instant we place our faith in Christ as Savior, we are forgiven of all sins—past, present, and future. There is not a sin in our lives that God cannot and does not forgive, because Christ's death released us from all sin debts.

Is confession necessary? Absolutely. The prodigal son recognized his waywardness and returned with a contrite and humble spirit. He verbalized his sorrow to his father. Yet, the father had already forgiven him, even before they tearfully met. "But while he was still a long way off, his father saw him and was filled with compassion for him" (Luke 15:20). We confess our sins, not to receive forgiveness, but to experience the cleansing and fellowship that we have missed in our disobedience.

Why do all the angels in heaven rejoice when a sinner is saved? Because a lost man or woman has been found by the grace and love of God, and his or her sins have been forgiven. There is nothing in heaven or on earth that brings as much joy as forgiveness.

God first forgives our sin; this is the primer. Then we are to forgive ourselves of the misery and pain we may have caused others. We move on to forgive others who have harmed and wounded us, for we forgive as God has forgiven us—liberally, freely, extravagantly.

The gospel is good news because God has taken away our sins and no longer holds them against us. We are a forgiven people who are called to celebrate the wonder of forgiveness by extending it to those around us who don't deserve it.

Spread the joy—celebrate forgiveness!

———— ❖ ————

I am so grateful for your forgiveness of my sins, Lord. I could never do enough good things to earn your pardon. It is simply your gift to me. You forgave me because you loved me and sent your Son to die on my behalf—in my place. Because I am forgiven, I have eternal hope and joy in my relationship with you. My guilt has been removed. Now that I am your child by faith in Christ, there is no sin that can keep your love from me.

Touchstone

Celebrate forgiveness

by accepting it yourself

and extending it

to others.

This is the day the LORD has made; let us rejoice and be glad in it.

PSALM 118:24

Choose Joy

———— ❖ ————

The trip had not gone exactly as Paul and Silas had anticipated, though the initial results were promising. They had established their beachhead on the European continent in the city of Philippi, a busy trade center in Macedonia. God had called them there (Acts 16:9–10), and people responded to the preaching of the gospel (v. 14). Then the bottom fell out. They were falsely accused, stripped, beaten by a hostile crowd, and tossed into the bowels of a prison.

The night was late when the duo, badly bruised and bloodied, did something rather strange—they began to sing hymns and worship God. Then an earthquake rumbled through the city, breaking the chains that held Paul and Silas tight. The responsible jailer, certain that they had escaped and fearful that he might lose his life, instead found them sitting composed in their cells. Such was their witness that the incredulous jailer invited them to his house, where he and his family accepted Christ.

Paul and Silas certainly didn't feel like singing. Their circumstances were rotten, and the prospects were grim. But they did something that every believer can do that will make an amazing difference—they chose joy.

You may remember Abraham Lincoln as the revered president of the United States. You may not know that at age nine he lost his mother; he was defeated in several election bids; he saw his twelve-year-old son Willie die; and he endured a painful marriage to an ambitious wife. Later Lincoln commented that "most men are about as happy as they choose to be."

Joy is a choice the believer in Christ can make regardless of the circumstances, since God's joy is never linked to our surroundings. Martin Luther said that "the heart of religion abides in the will," and that is never more true than when it comes to our experience of God's joy.

We can choose joy because God commends it as our best option. Sure, we can elect to be bitter or angry or discouraged, but where will it get us? Is there any profit to yielding to emotions or persuasions that are innately debilitating? The believer can choose God's joy because he always makes it available to his servants. Our situation may be hostile, depressing, and demoralizing, but the joy of the Lord is ours for the choosing.

Choosing joy in our straits means we decide to completely trust God. David frequently felt as though God was distant, and he even considered the appealing notion of running away from his problems (Psalm 55:4–8). Yet in the end, David consistently concluded that, despite his troubles, he would trust God (v. 23). When we choose joy we are deciding to walk by faith, not by sight, and it is faith that God rewards and blesses.

Choosing joy means we choose to glorify God in our lives, commit to spend time in Scripture, purpose to forgive those who aggrieve us, believe that all things work together for good, and decide to depend on the resident power of the Holy Spirit within us.

Whatever your problems, you can make a decision of the will, enabled by the grace and Spirit of Christ, that will turn you toward the joy of the Lord. God has shown you the way of joy in his Word. Choose it today.

———— ◦ ————

Father, thank you for making it possible for me to choose joy in my circumstances. Thank you that I can choose it right now and trust you to enable me to experience it as I surrender to your loving care and provision. I may not feel like singing, but I want to have your joy in my life. Create praise in my heart that I may see you at work.

Touchstone

Joy is always
the right choice.

Get rid of all bitterness, rage and anger.

EPHESIANS 4:31

Dealing with Anger

———— ⊕ ————

King Saul was chosen by God to lead the nation of Israel. He apparently had all the right physical and mental characteristics (1 Samuel 9:1–3), and initially he met with success. Spiritually, however, his heart was not loyal to God, and the Lord rejected his leadership. Instead God selected a young shepherd boy named David as the future king.

When I think of Saul, I am struck with the portrait of an angry man. David's heroics and heart for God gained the admiration of Israelites while Saul degenerated into bitterness and rage, resulting in misery and treachery.

Anger is the extreme enemy of joy. They cannot coexist. When we are upset with God, ourselves, others, or our present predicament, we are vulnerable to other leeches of joy, such as depression and discouragement. Our inner turmoil makes it virtually impossible to enjoy life.

Everyone struggles with anger on some level. We all occasionally lose our composure in a heated moment. We are legitimately disturbed over injustice and unfairness. We all get mad. This is not the kind of anger that is dangerous. What is ominous is the internal seething over our problems or relationships that colors all we do, think, or say. We become consumed with abiding hostility.

There is a way of escape. We are not captives of sin, which includes anger. The first and most important step is to honestly admit our anger to God. He is never threatened or disappointed when we are honest with him. David was frequently annoyed with the many problems he faced, and the psalms record many of his vexations. David learned, however, to talk to the Lord about his anger. "I pour out my complaint before him; before him I tell my trouble" (Psalm 142:2). God knows the anger that rests inside you, so why not tell him? There is great relief in admitting your anger to God and discovering that he is willing to listen and help.

Having brought your anger into the open with God, ask him to help you think through the reasons for your animosity. Let him help you get to the root of your problem. You may be mad today over something that happened long ago. You may be angry with yourself, but are taking it out on someone else.

When the root of your anger is found, ask the Lord to forgive you.

Again, understand I am addressing the anger that has grown into an emotional cancer, not mere irritation. We can be angry and not sin (Ephesians 4:26). Yet, nothing less than admission, confession, and repentance will work against the advanced stage of anger. At this level, God must do the healing, and he is able to with your cooperation.

Remember that deep-rooted anger is a conscious decision you make in response to your circumstances. You need to make a different choice—to trust God and turn to him for solutions. The problems that made you angry won't disappear, but you can respond with a completely new attitude, and your joy will be restored.

---------- ● ----------

Father, I realize I need you to help me honestly look at the anger in my heart. Let your Spirit show me if I have harbored angry thoughts and feelings about others or about events in my life that have brought me pain. With your leadership, bring me into confession and repentance so I may experience your joy and cleansing. Rule in my heart with your peace and give me the emotional well-being that comes from your gentle, healing touch.

Touchstone

Deal constructively with
anger before it deals
destructively with you.

Drink from your river of delights.

PSALM 36:8

Delighting in the Lord

Richard Baxter was a Puritan pastor in the seventeenth century who spent much of his difficult life in sickness and trial, spending eighteen months in an English prison for his faith during his later years. Despite his trials, he was one of the most prolific Christian writers and passionate preachers of his day.

The power for Baxter's faith and the strength for his ministry came from the same source that we can tap into today. Baxter wrote of this compelling motivation: "May the Living God, who is the portion and rest of the saints, make these our carnal minds so spiritual, and our earthly hearts so heavenly, that loving him, and delighting in him, may be the work of our lives."

Richard Baxter delighted in the Lord. His joy and zeal for knowing and preaching Christ was founded in a deep delight in the person of God. The psalmist tells us to "delight [ourselves] in the LORD" (Psalm 37:4). While many are afraid of God, and others believe he is an angry deity, Christians alone can experience the wonder of actually making God their chief enjoyment. As David celebrated by dancing before the Lord, our hearts can leap with joy over the pleasure of knowing the most marvelous person in heaven and earth—Jesus Christ.

We delight in Christ by gaining a deeper appreciation of his character. God is gracious and kind. He is merciful and forgiving. He is faithful and generous. He is our friend and helper. As we think on these and other aspects of God's personality and attributes, we will find ourselves with thankful and grateful hearts—both systematically and spontaneously. Feasting on the character of God, the kind of person he really is, fills our souls with growing and mysterious wonder. We can never exhaust the riches of his ways and personhood, and he becomes the joy and delight of our hearts even in trying times. God wants us to delight in him, and he relishes in revealing the glory of his being to us.

Our delight in the person of Christ centers on a profound respect and love for the Scriptures. "His delight is in the law of the LORD, and on his law he meditates day and night" (Psalm 1:2). We cannot find our delight in Christ apart from rejoicing in the truth of his Word. The Bible is the revelation of God, which enlightens our minds and hearts with the right knowledge of him. We come to the Word with rich expectation and anticipation that God will speak personally to us. We trust God to fulfill his promises.

Can you think of anyone you would rather know more intimately than Jesus Christ? Can you accept his invitation—his command—to delight yourself in him so the deepest desires of your heart are met by him? Drink from the river of his delights, and you will find that delighting in God can become the most pleasurable work of your life.

———— • ————

It's thrilling to know how much you delight in me, Lord, and how eager you are for me to delight in you. You have so much more in mind for me than I can possibly ever imagine. Your plans are for my welfare and bounty, and your thoughts toward me are exceedingly wondrous. May I awaken to the amazing truth that you take great pleasure in me and my fellowship with you. And may I learn to delight in you in increasing measure.

Touchstone

God is honored and you
are blessed when you
delight chiefly in him.

In God I trust; I will not be afraid. What can man do to me?

PSALM 56:11

Difficult People

---- ◉ ----

If there was a Top Ten list of joy's most virulent foes, conflict with others would indisputably rank near the top. Relationship woes at work, in the family, and around the neighborhood contribute significantly to our unhappiness. Dealing with the people that spoil our joy is hard enough; handling our thoughts about them is even harder. Sometimes the conflict is so severe that our lives descend into a bog of perpetual anger. We're stuck being around these people; we've had about as much as we can take, and we really don't know what to do about it.

My initial years at First Baptist Church of Atlanta placed me in an explosive situation where I had to depend on God's help in dealing with my emotions. Tensions among the deacons ran so high that one actually struck me during a worship service. Half of the church members left over some disagreements, and I constantly had to deal with relationships that were strained.

I did not discover any quick and easy solutions, but God did help me. He promises us a joyful life (John 10:10), and he provides us with the wisdom and strength we need to deal with difficult people.

The most important step we can take each day is to turn toward joy. When we came to Christ for salvation, we turned from our sin and to the Savior. Turning toward joy is a deliberate, daily decision to seek the joy of the Lord in our lives. It's also a conscious, ongoing choice not to allow the actions of others to become the focus of our thinking. Are we going to concentrate on and repeatedly mull over what others are doing to us, or will we turn resolutely to the Lord? When the inappropriate and hateful words and deeds of others drive us to turn toward the Lord, they can actually be unwitting agents of joy. If we make the choice to turn toward joy and not anger or bitterness, we lay the groundwork for triumph.

We must also learn to take refuge in the Lord. Pursued intensely by King Saul, David found comfort, peace, and joy by taking refuge in God. The Lord became David's hiding place (Psalm 32:7). Taking refuge in the Lord means that we ask him to be our protection and defense. We commit ourselves to his safekeeping, knowing that he is the only one who can safeguard us from the schemes and barbs of people. Praying specifically about our problem and staying in the Word of God are the most practical ways we can find our shelter in the storm.

Having turned toward joy and taken refuge in Christ, we must daily entrust ourselves and live uprightly. Will he deliver us from those who make our lives miserable, bring us to a new job, move us to a new town? Perhaps, but the outcome must be placed squarely in the Lord's hands. "So then, those who suffer according to God's will should commit themselves to their faithful Creator and continue to do good" (1 Peter 4:19). God will not let you bear more than you can handle. He will help you. Don't let the person who troubles your soul keep you from a life committed to righteousness and joy. Keep doing good, even to those who persecute you, and God will ultimately reward you.

Think upon Christ, who "when they hurled their insults at him, he did not retaliate; when he suffered, he made no threats. Instead, he entrusted himself to him who judges justly" (1 Peter 2:23). God will exalt you as you refuse to strike back and rest your case with him.

Jesus, you had to deal with difficult people during your earthly ministry. You were harassed, tested, scorned, and falsely accused, yet you continued to preach the good news of salvation to all. Since you live in me through the person of the Holy Spirit, I ask for your help to handle those relationships that simply are too arduous for me to negotiate. Make me more than a conqueror through your great love and power.

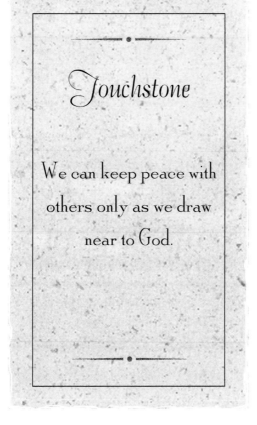

Touchstone

We can keep peace with others only as we draw near to God.

Come, all you who are thirsty, come to the waters.

ISAIAH 55:1

Fresh Encounters with God

Jacob was not exactly on great terms with the Lord when he wrestled with the Lord and came away with a new attitude. Moses had roamed the desert for forty years when he came upon a burning bush and heard God's voice. Isaiah had a vision of God's holy character and came away with a rich reverence for Jehovah. All had fresh encounters with the Lord that resulted in a renewed understanding of themselves and God.

Joy doesn't ride well on the coattails of the past. Fond memories are just that and do little to bring us the realization of God's joy for today. We can't rely solely on prior experiences—authentic as they may be—to sustain our daily walk with Christ.

This is why fresh encounters with the Lord are vital for ongoing joy. By a fresh encounter, I mean a relational experience with the Savior that renews and refreshes our soul. Let's face it—our personal relationship with Jesus can grow stale, set in routine or tradition, lacking spiritual vitality. The tyranny of the urgent can numb our hunger and thirst for intimacy with Christ. Knowing God as our first love can become a distant memory.

If you are in need of a fresh touch from the Lord, the most important step you can take is to spend some quality time with the Lord. You obviously cannot program the ministry of the Holy Spirit in your life—he is free to work anytime—but he certainly has ample opportunity when you give him your full attention.

Freely admit you haven't sensed his presence in your life as you once did. You can't fool the Lord. You have to be completely honest and drop any rationalization.

Don't come with any agenda other than to hear what the Lord has to say. You never know what he has in mind. He may lead you to Scriptures that speak to your soul about matters you have never considered. He knows what your soul needs to be restored. God took the initiative to send his Son to die on our behalf, and he certainly is willing to take the initiative in renewing your fellowship with him. Be quiet. Be still. Listen. And let God speak through his Word, a book, a hymn.

Realize that seeds of joy may be planted in your heart for growth at the proper time. Sometimes we spend time with the Lord and don't seem to come away changed. Don't worry; God is in the life-changing business, and your time with him today may lay the groundwork for wonders next week or next month.

You can be sure that if you seek the Lord and come to him for a fresh touch, he will hear and answer. He knows when our weary souls need to be replenished and longs for intimacy with us even more than we do with him.

As long as you desire to walk in fellowship with Christ, you will find many fresh encounters along the way, each lovingly designed to bring you into deeper worship and knowledge of him and to give you ever increasing joy.

He has already made the first move through the gift of his Son and his Spirit. It's your move today.

———— ◆ ————

I realize that I need a fresh encounter with you, O Lord. I seem to operate on autopilot too much of the time, moving in the realm of the comfortable and convenient. Open my spiritual eyes to behold your wonder and help me to see anew. Don't let me live in the past, but draw me into new vistas of your grace for today, your loving provision and plan for my adventure of faith.

Touchstone

A fresh encounter with
God may be just the new
beginning you need.

I say these things while I am still in the world, so that
they may have the full measure of my joy within them.

JOHN 17:13

Fullness of Joy

In the few days before his crucifixion, Jesus talked intimately with his disciples about many compelling subjects. Knowing that his journey to the cross was about to be consummated and his brief time with the disciples ended, he wanted them to remember essential truths that would sustain them after his ascension. Not surprisingly, he talked a good bit about joy.

Joy is inseparable from obedience and God's love. "If you obey my commands, you will remain in my love, just as I have obeyed my Father's commands and remain in his love. I have told you this so that my joy may be in you and that your joy may be complete" (John 15:10–11). The more we do what God plainly tells us to do in Scripture, the greater our joy. Obedience to biblical principles is the spiritual architecture for ongoing joy. That's why obedience isn't drudgery; it's living in the framework of God's love and joy. Jesus' obedience to the Father is our example.

Joy is inseparable from the power of the Resurrection. The disciples' grief would "turn to joy" (John 16:20) when they saw him in his resurrection glory. Part of our joy is knowing that we too will see Jesus in his transcendent glory. The Lord has prepared a place for us to live with him forever in heaven. We will be with him. All mourning and suffering will cease, and joy will permanently reign. The hope of the Resurrection is the solid bedrock for lasting joy.

Joy is inseparable from a life of prayer founded on the sufficiency of Christ. "Until now you have not asked for anything in my name. Ask and you will receive, and your joy will be complete" (John 16:24). Prayer is asking God to meet our needs in his wisdom and his timing. It is the practical forum for expressing our dependence on Christ in the details of life—watching how God answers our petitions, deepens our faith, and completes our joy. God hears. God is able. God answers. We are humbled, grateful, and delighted in the Lord's care for our lives.

Joy is inseparable from a life of unity. "Holy Father, protect them by the power of your name ... so that they may be one as we are one" (John 17:11). Joy abounds when we live in harmony and peace with others in the body of Christ. Our witness to the world is a church bound together by Christ. Such a church joyfully proclaims the love of Christ to a world divided and torn by sin.

The Lord of joy wants to make our joy complete. This is what he wanted his disciples to unequivocally know and what he promises to every follower today. His joy is completely ours.

Thank you, Jesus, for the joy that was in your heart even as the cross drew near. Thank you for sharing your truth about how I might receive and abide in your joy, especially as I live in obedience to your Word and come consistently to you in prayer. I pray you would help me to experience the fullness of your joy this day and in the days to come.

Touchstone

Jesus has given us all
we need for complete joy.

Come, let us rejoice in him.

PSALM 66:6

Rejoice!

The apostle Paul wanted the fledging church at Philippi to hear the message loud and clear: "Rejoice in the Lord always. I will say it again: Rejoice!" (Philippians 4:4). Paul wanted the believers to be happy. It wasn't a mere suggestion or wishful thinking; it was a command.

Who doesn't want to be marked by a cheerful nature? Other than occasional, normal bouts with melancholy, no one cares to be depressed. We are more productive, more optimistic, and more helpful to others when our spirits are joyful.

Thankfully, the apostle who espoused joy also gave the Philippians (and us) the Lord's insight on cultivating a life that rejoices in the Lord in the verses that followed his injunction.

"Let your gentleness be evident to all. The Lord is near" (Philippians 4:5). Joy is virtually impossible to experience when we are at odds with one another. Even one sour relationship at the office can make good work miserable. A rift with a neighbor breeds ill will and an uneasy spirit.

Paul's advice in our relationships with each other is the sure but hard route to peace and joy—be gentle and forbearing in all our dealings. Some have translated this as "sweet reasonableness." In other words, don't be demanding. When offended, don't strike back, or return evil for evil (1 Peter 3:9). This response is impossible for people alone, but very possible for those who yield to the life of the Holy Spirit. Can we really love our enemies? Can we really do good to those who torment or persecute us? Can we actually pray for those who plot against us? The answer is yes, but only as we set our hearts to obey the Lord through the Spirit's enabling. When we do, the gentleness that Paul describes descends on our homes, our workplaces, our communities, our churches. Led by the Spirit, we defer our rights and entrust ourselves to the Lord's protection.

The other key to rejoicing is taking everything to the Lord in prayer. "Do not be anxious about anything, but in everything, by prayer and petition, with thanksgiving, present your requests to God" (Philippians 4:6).

Our lives become burdensome and our hearts sorrowful when we strive to solve our problems our own way, without calling on God for help. Once we learn that God cares about every detail of our existence and that he actually wants us to talk to him about our needs, we learn to rejoice, even in difficulty.

Do you have a problem or need? Take it to God in prayer, thank him that he hears, and trust him to bring about his solution in his time. He doesn't want you to fret or worry, but desires you to pray.

Rejoice in the Lord. Be gentle in your affairs with others. Go quickly to the Lord with your concerns in prayer. And rejoice in the Lord.

———— • ————

Dear Lord, I need your help to allow your joy to reign in my relationships. I want your "sweet reasonableness" to flow through me to others. May your gentle and quiet Spirit keep me in touch with your boundless joy.

Touchstone

A gentle spirit and a
prayerful heart are
essential ingredients for
a joyful life.

He will guard the feet of his saints.

God's Keeping Power

---

*C*an you remember the times when as a small child you felt safe and secure in the presence of a parent? When you were afraid of the dark, you climbed into your parents' bed and slept soundly. When you stepped off of the school bus after the first day of school, someone special was waiting for you.

Now that you are an adult, your anxieties aren't so quickly or easily put away. The pressures of the job and the uncertainties of the future work incessantly to keep you nervous and uneasy.

There is a facet of your relationship with Jesus Christ that can help anchor your emotions and feelings in the steadfast love of God. The God who saved you and lives in you is also the God who keeps you. The idea in the Greek and Hebrew is similar: God is watching over us, protecting us, holding on to us.

The psalmist expresses the comfort that comes from sensing and embracing God's keeping power: "He will not let your foot slip—he who watches over you will not slumber; indeed, he who watches over Israel will neither slumber nor sleep. . . . The Lord will watch over your coming and going both now and forevermore" (Psalm 121:3–4, 8).

God keeps us *from* certain evils and calamities. When the ancient king Abimelech had taken Abraham's wife, Sarah, from him after Abraham lied and told the king she was his sister, God kept the sincere king from sinning against him (Genesis 20:1–6). David's motive was strictly vengeful when he angrily steamed toward Nathan's home to kill him until David was persuaded by Nathan's wife, Abigail, to refrain from his hotheaded pursuit. "May you be blessed for your good judgment," David thanked

Abigail, "and for keeping me from bloodshed this day and from avenging myself with my own hands" (1 Samuel 25:33). God keeps us out of harm's way more often than we know.

The comfort of Scripture is more than God merely keeping us away from problems; the real consolation comes from knowing that God keeps us *in* difficult and demanding circumstances.

God keeps us strong when we are weak. He keeps us patient when we are restless. He keeps us steadfast when we are faltering. In the midst of strife, God is the one who keeps us. We are, as Peter wrote, "shielded by God's power until the coming of the salvation that is ready to be revealed in the last time" (1 Peter 1:5). This is why we can "greatly rejoice, though now for a little while [we] may have had to suffer grief in all kinds of trials" (v. 6).

God keeps us through his power and faithfulness. God keeps his word. His promises do not fail. He will do what he says if we put our trust in him. No danger that threatens is greater than his power. He is the covenant keeping God, who has pledged to never leave or forsake us.

Our Father in heaven is the one we can run to for safekeeping. He is the strong tower, the place of refuge, who will guard our souls until we see him face-to-face.

Whenever I feel weak and frail, remind me, Lord, that your grip on my life is firm and secure. I am kept by your power and love, and that power is greater than all my trials. I praise you, for what you have begun in my life, you will complete, because you are so faithful. I worship you.

Touchstone

We are kept in God's
unfailing love by his
faithfulness and power.

And my God will meet all your needs according to his glorious riches in Christ Jesus.

PHILIPPIANS 4:19

God Is Good

In the twenty-eighth chapter of Deuteronomy is a chilling narrative of God's dealing with the nation of Israel as they prepared to finally move into the land of Canaan after forty years of walking in circles.

The pronouncement of God's blessings that are contingent on the Hebrews' obedience is heartening. As long as they sought the Lord and followed his commands, the people would experience a wonderful life—blessed in the home, on the land, in battle, and as a nation. On the other hand, if they did not obey, curses would multiply—disease, famine, defeat, and pain.

We now live in the age of God's grace extended through the sacrificial death of Christ, but we still face the consequences that stem from disobedience. And we can learn pointed lessons from the Hebrews' behavior that can motivate us to a life of joyful discipleship.

After clearly listing the distasteful repercussions of rebellion, Moses plainly states the surprising rationale for disobedience. They would suffer in coming days because they did not "serve the LORD your God joyfully and gladly" (Deuteronomy 28:47). Their journey into bondage would come when they looked to someone other than Jehovah for their delight and satisfaction.

Ultimately, our failure to follow Jesus is a lack of confidence in the goodness of God. God promises to supply all our needs (Philippians 4:19). He assures us that if we make his kingdom a priority in our lives, we need not fret and fume over the basic necessities of life (Matthew 6:24–34). When we doubt God's goodness to meet the fundamental demands of our existence—physical and spiritual—we are apt to seek our satisfaction in pursuits that can never fully gratify.

The innate goodness of God is crucial to a life of continued joy. God is always good to his people. There is never a moment in time when God is not working for our best interest, even if that entails some unpleasant discipline (Hebrews 12:10). Our personal repentance from sin is made possible by the goodness and kindness of the Lord (Romans 2:4).

A joyful Christian obeys Christ, not because it is his duty (although this is true), but because he knows that God's goodness is behind all his commands. We serve the Lord with a joyful heart for he gives us all things out of his hand.

If life is less than satisfying at this time, ask yourself if you are looking to the Lord. Are you eagerly and expectantly seeking Christ to supply all your needs, or have you turned to someone or something else to bring you joy?

God has one answer: Seek him for the abundance of all things and you will never be disappointed. It's the surest path to God's blessings.

It's so easy to forget how good you are to me, Lord. I praise you that your goodness is always seeking me out so I never need to yield to fear and anxiety. I thank you that you are good all the time, every day, in every way. All good things come from you, most importantly, the gift of your Son, Jesus Christ, my Savior, Lord, and life.

Touchstone

We serve the Lord
joyfully as we put
our confidence in his
goodness.

And he will be called Wonderful Counselor, Mighty God, Everlasting Father, Prince of Peace.

ISAIAH 9:6

Great Joy

———————— ❖ ————————

*T*he heavens had been silent for almost four hundred years. The word of the Lord had not been heard since the days of the prophets, but this was about to change.

To disbelieving Zechariah, the angel Gabriel spoke of his son's upcoming birth: "He will be a joy and delight to you, and many will rejoice because of his birth" (Luke 1:14). To amazed Mary, Gabriel had this wonderful news: "You have found favor with God. You will be with child and give birth to a son, and you are to give him the name Jesus" (vv. 30–31). Soon after, amid the darkness of a shepherd's night, the angel delivered the long awaited news: "I bring you good news of great joy that will be for all the people. Today in the town of David a Savior has been born to you; he is Christ the Lord" (Luke 2:10–11).

Conceived in the mind of God for all eternity, the birth of Christ was now reality. The Incarnation, God becoming flesh in the person of his Son, Jesus Christ, had finally come. The Anointed One was crying in a Bethlehem feeding trough, and it was a time for rejoicing.

Two thousand years later, the great joy has not diminished. The Good News has not lost any of its appeal. Christ our Savior has come; he lived, died for our sins, rose from the grave, and ascended to the Father.

No longer are we who put our faith in him in bondage. Our sins have been forgiven, and we have been liberated from the yoke of death. We have been reconciled to God. We who were once enemies of God are now his friends.

We have been rescued from a life of emptiness, striving to find purpose and satisfaction in vain pursuits. Now, because of the Savior, we have a relationship with God himself, enjoying all the pleasures of intimacy with the Father. Reconciled with him, Christ is our Wonderful Counselor, guiding, teaching, and caring.

We are saved from despair and hopelessness. In our darkest moments, the Light of the World is in our bosom, bringing us inexplicable hope. The Prince of Peace lives within to give us tranquillity in the fiercest of storms. He is Immanuel, God with us, for us, in us forever.

The Savior loves us with everlasting love. We are never outside his extravagant mercy and love, never beyond the reach of his grace. The great news of redemption is that we don't have to earn the love of the Savior; he gives it to us freely as we come to him.

The Savior of the world has come for you. Mighty God has come to live in you, love through you, fill your spirit with himself, and give you every reason for great joy in this world and the next.

———— ◆ ————

Jesus, you are the joy of my life. I live each day with the Good News abiding in my heart in your indwelling presence. I have been rescued from the penalty and power of sin and given the gift of your righteousness for all eternity. I rejoice in God my Savior.

Touchstone

We have every reason
for joy, because we have
Jesus Christ in us, for us,
and with us.

Light is shed upon the righteous and joy on the upright in heart.

PSALM 97:11

Joy in the Journey

We are a driven people. We set goals, establish objectives, and find the most efficient means to move from point A to point B. We are prone to be preoccupied with the destination—the goal reached, the plan consummated.

While the Bible certainly commends the person who plans wisely and works hard, it doesn't imply that such deliberate focus excludes the ability to enjoy the journey along the way.

One of the most wonderful aspects of Christian joy is that it can be experienced day after day. It is not reserved for the pinnacle of personal achievement, but can be delightfully discovered in the routine, the mundane, the most pedestrian of days.

Think about it: Are you so fixed on obtaining that specialized degree, securing that anticipated promotion, waiting for that special person to come into your life that you have been oblivious to the daily delights that God has set in your determined path? Have you become so obsessed with the destination that the journey passes along with monotonous drudgery? The Danish philosopher Søren Kierkegaard remarked, "Most men pursue pleasure with such breathless haste, that they hurry past it."

Relishing God's joy in our journey stems from recognizing that each and every day is a gift from him. We rightfully prepare for the future, but plainly realize that our times are in his hands. We really are frail and feeble people whose best laid plans can be all too suddenly derailed. We can't take tomorrow for granted, so we had better look to the Lord for the joy he has to grant today. This is the thrust of James's exhortation: "Now listen, you who say, 'Today or tomorrow we will go to this or that city, spend a year there, carry on business and make money.' Why, you do not even know what will happen tomorrow" (James 4:13–14). This should not only help us guard against presumption but should also stimulate us to enjoy the days God graciously gives us.

Learning to see God at work in the small as well as the big occasions of life makes plenty of room for joy as well. Playing with the kids in the front yard, walking around the block with our spouse, gathering around the television for a good movie— these are the times when we can learn to enjoy God's good gifts and celebrate his participating presence in our lives. If we rely exclusively on the significant achievements of life for joy, we will overlook thousands of seemingly insignificant moments that God has provided for our enjoyment—a smile, a good meal, a chat with a friend.

Keep the big picture and celebrate when you reach your goal. There is a definite thrill when you finish what you set out to do, but remember to enjoy the trip along the way. After all, God is with you every step of the way.

———— ◈ ————

I admit, Lord, that I am so often in a hurry that I don't enjoy the blessings along the way. Help me to slow down, to trust you, and to relish the relationships, opportunities, and challenges of each and every day. You give me all good things to enjoy; don't let my worries and fears keep me from seeing your hand at work in the ordinary details I tend to overlook. I thank you because I belong to you.

Touchstone

The journey is just
as important as the
destination.

You will be like a well-watered garden, like a spring whose waters never fail.

ISAIAH 58:11

Joy Runs Deep

tanding on a boat dock near a favorite lake of mine, I could see the wind ripple the waters, blowing them toward me. Farther out in the channel, however, a boat with its motor cut was drifting in a different direction. The strong breeze made its mark on the lake's surface, but the stronger channel current governed the flow.

I often have thought about that scene when I consider the joy of the Lord. We are easily swayed by the superficial events of our lives, the happenings of the day, the words spoken about us. I can remember a time in an early pastorate when I was spending weeks fixating on a unkind remark by another pastor. Later, a hospital visit to a very ill parishioner helped me realize how insignificant the remark really was.

True joy isn't affected by the winds of chance and circumstance. Genuine joy—God's joy—runs deep beneath the clutter of our experiences and stays the course. The key is learning to rely on that deep source of holy joy in the midst of adversity. When we do, we tap into the inexhaustible, steadfast power of God in a life-changing way.

The deep flow of God's joy is ours when we learn to practice his presence. Throughout the Old Testament, people took courage in difficult straits because they were promised the presence of Jehovah in their trials. "Do not be terrified," God told Joshua, "for the LORD your God will be with you wherever you go" (Joshua 1:9). David knew that his joy came from God's presence (Psalm 16:11). God's presence is practiced as we do everything as "unto the Lord," daily commune with him through prayer and Scripture, and rely exclusively on the person of the Holy Spirit for our wisdom and strength.

God's deep joy is readily encountered when we put Christ, not our problems, at the center of our lives. What is your focus as you go through the day—Christ or your troubles? When you get up in the morning or retire at night, is your mind centered on Christ or your problems? The Bible tells us to "set [our] minds on things above, not on earthly things" (Colossians 3:2). This means we have a mind-set of a fixed focus of faith in Christ as we go about our day. We tackle our problems, but from a mind and heart that sees Christ as the problem solver. Nothing is too difficult for him.

We also can live in the constant stream of God's joy as we set our hearts on pleasing him rather than people. The apostle Paul said it was his "goal to please [Christ]" (2 Corinthians 5:9). The person who is bent on pleasing God is able to know the unchanging joy of Christ because he doesn't look to his circumstances or the people around him for his fulfillment. If our ambition is to please the Lord, we respond to rough remarks with a gentle spirit, tackle adversity with faith, and extend forgiveness to those who wrong us.

Don't let the fickle winds of temporal circumstances determine the quality of your joy. Remember that deep within your soul is the determinant of all real joy—the person of Jesus Christ. Practice his presence, live with him at the center of your will and emotions, and seek to please him in all you do.

———— • ————

I do see, Lord, that your joy is at the center of a satisfied life, wholly independent of my circumstances. Teach me to have a fixed focus of faith in you so that I am not carried off course by upsetting circumstances. May your joy run deep into my soul so that I am anchored in you.

Touchstone

God's joy is the steady
and consistent center
of abundant living.

My souls finds rest in God alone.

PSALM 62:1

Restful Joy

———— ❦ ————

*S*t. Augustine was the first who noticed something different in the Bible's description of the seventh day of Creation. The first six days, Augustine observed, were marked by the defining words, "there was evening, and there was morning." The seventh day lacked the descriptive phrase.

The distinction is clarified in the fourth chapter of Hebrews. The seventh day was the day when God rested from his works, enjoying the splendor of his creative masterpiece. The respite is more than just symbolic for the believer; there is dramatic spiritual significance. "There remains, then, a Sabbath-rest for the people of God; for anyone who enters God's rest also rests from his own work, just as God did from his" (Hebrews 4:9–10).

God has engineered a lifestyle pinned on a keen sense of his provision and faithfulness. He does not want us to be people of continual worry and work, unable to recognize his peaceful and joyful presence in our midst. The Sabbath-rest is an everyday preoccupation with the sufficiency of Christ. F. B. Meyer explains this when he wrote: "We must remember to maintain within our hearts the spirit of Sabbath calm and peace, not fussy, not anxious, nor fretful nor impetuous, refraining our feet from our own paths, our hand from our devices, refusing to make our own joy and do our own works. It is only when we are fully resolved to act thus, allowing God to originate his own plans and to work in us for their accomplishment that we enter into rest."

This relaxed, composed life that should mark the Christian comes only through faith. And that faith can only come through a growing conviction that God cares enough to take care of us.

We have to work, think, plan, pray, and practice all the other disciplines the Bible clearly endorses. And yet behind all of our preparation is the wonderful awareness of God's adequacy. All our striving would be losing if God did not come through on our behalf.

God's rest, which continually refreshes our joy and stamina, is the knowledge that God does have it all figured out, even when we obviously don't. We cannot forecast the future. We cannot tell where the next week or month will take us. Even our best efforts can be nullified by events beyond our sphere of influence, but nothing is beyond the scope of God's providence. When we commit our works and thoughts to him, he will orchestrate their results for our good.

Resting from the futility of complete dependence on our self-effort is hard work. We must make "every effort to enter that rest" (Hebrews 4:11), refusing to be snared by the relentless unease and anxiety that infects our culture, placing serene confidence in God's love and power.

Start every project, begin every day, tackle every challenge with the assurance that God is the prime mover. God himself will see us through.

———— ◆ ————

I come today to rest in your love for me. I relax in your providential provision and protection. I know that you have created me for your own good pleasure and that my times are in your hands. I cease fretting and fussing, recognizing that my complaints betray your goodness to me. You are my complete sufficiency.

Touchstone

When we rest in the Lord,

we make great spiritual

progress.

Being confident of this, that he who began a good
work in you will carry it on to completion.

PHILIPPIANS 1:6

Just Do It

od is keen on getting the job done. The Savior came to earth and will come again because God has decreed it. Jesus said he glorified the Father in heaven "by completing the work you gave me to do" (John 17:4). When the Lord decides to do something, you can bet he will get it done: "What I have said, that will I bring about; what I have planned, that will I do" (Isaiah 46:11).

To his children, God has given the same sense of satisfaction when a task is finished, a project completed, an objective reached. "Hope deferred makes the heart sick, but a longing fulfilled is a tree of life" (Proverbs 13:12). Always coming up short eventually breeds discouragement and frustration, but seeing the tangible fruits of our labor is very rewarding.

After several adventurous years of seeking a river passage from the Mississippi to the Pacific coast, William Clark wrote in his diary as he heard the ocean's roar, "Ocean in view; Oh, the joy." The waterway Lewis and Clark sought did not exist, but they had reached their goal.

The essential element of discovering the joy of accomplishment is working within the fulfilling framework of God's will. Jesus could say he did what honored his Father because his priority was "to do the will of him who sent me and to finish his work" (John 4:34). There were many towns Jesus didn't visit, plenty of people he didn't heal or save. He did what was on the Father's agenda. The greatest purpose you can have is to always be about the Lord's work. All it takes is a humble heart that says each day, "Lord, I'm available to do your work today. I don't know what that may be, but I trust you to accomplish your good pleasure in and through me."

The next important step is faithfulness in the daily rounds. Accomplishment is often lacking because we fail to stay faithful in the details. In the parable of the talents, the successful servant is rewarded for his diligence with God's provision. "Well done, good and faithful servant! You have been faithful with a few things; I will put you in charge of many things. Come and share your master's happiness!" (Matthew 25:21).

We will also have to do battle with the inimitable foes of accomplishment—procrastination and fear. Procrastination keeps us from enjoying God's good plans for us. We put so many things off for so long that we seldom taste the sweetness of success. We crave, but never do. Fear of failure, fear of rejection, fear in any form likewise inhibits our joy because we don't exercise the faith that propels us into God's joy of an accomplished life.

Whether or not you accomplish great or little things isn't the issue at all. God has a specific purpose for your existence, and you have to cooperate with his plans. Just start with something small but measurable—read the Bible for five minutes a day for a week, write one encouraging letter to a friend—and watch the excitement build.

You may think you can't do it. You have waited too long, wasted too many years. Your fears still loom large. But in God's scheme of grace and forgiveness, it's never too late to do the right thing. You can do "everything through him who gives [you] strength" (Philippians 4:13).

———— • ————

I am available to you today, Lord, that you may accomplish your will through me. I thank you that you desire to see success in my life in your way and in your timing and that you understand the desires of my heart. Give me boldness to do what I know to be your will and daily grace to persevere so I may be your good hand at work.

Touchstone

God is at work in us to do
his work through us.

But you would be fed with the finest of wheat; with
honey from the rock I would satisfy you.

PSALM 81:16

Let God Choose

⸻ ✦ ⸻

J oy seldom settles in the midst of the tension and strife or in the caldron of covetousness. We usually want more, not less, and we want it now.

Abraham and Lot confronted the raw power of a covetous spirit when their herds and belongings created a volatile situation. The land they had migrated to from Egypt was unable to sustain the livestock operations of all of the relatives. Some heated quarrels had broken out among the hired hands until Abraham stepped in with a solution.

"Let's not have any quarreling between you and me, or between your herdsmen and mine, for we are brothers. Is not the whole land before you? Let's part company. If you go to the left, I'll go to the right; if you go to the right, I'll go to the left" (Genesis 13:8–9).

Lot looked around at the fertile plain that lay east and scored what appeared to be a big coup. Abraham stayed in the land of Canaan. Who won? Well, Lot's journey took him toward Sodom, where he was captured by raiding parties until Abraham rescued him. Later, the angel of the Lord would have to deliver Lot from the wickedness of the city.

As it turned out, Abraham made the best choice even though it initially appeared that Lot had seized the day. The great patriarch had driven the fatal stake into the heart of a covetous spirit—he surrendered his rights to the Lord.

"God always gives his best to those who leave the choice with him," wrote missionary Jim Elliot, who was martyred in the jungles of South America. Abraham did just that—he yielded his natural impulses for self-determination to the Lord. And did God ever reward him! "The LORD said to Abram after Lot had parted from him, 'Lift up your eyes from where are and look north and south, east and west. All the land that you see I will give to you and your offspring forever'" (Genesis 13:14–15).

What is it that you want badly right now? More money? A more prestigious title or a prized promotion? Do you lay around at night thinking about how you can make it happen? Are you so caught up in pursuing your own agenda that you have failed to ask the Lord what he thinks about it all?

Try letting God choose for you. This means putting the matter before him in prayer, being honest about your feelings and ambitions, but leaving the decision in his hands. Will God give anything other than his best? Isn't it better to trust in his definition of what's best than in your own?

When we resolve to allow God to supply our need and refuse to manipulate the circumstances, we come to a place where joy and contentment take over. Stress and anxiety dissolve, because we have placed the choice into the hands of our omniscient, omnipotent, omnipresent Father, who will give nothing less than the absolute best thing.

———— ◉ ————

It's true, Father, that even when I doubt you, you have the best possible plan for my life. I release my possessive grip on my own agenda and surrender my ambitions to you, trusting in your wisdom and power. This is the best decision I can possibly make.

Touchstone

When we let God choose,

we always receive

his best.

You have loved righteousness and hated wickedness;
therefore God, your God, has set you above your
companions by anointing you with the oil of joy.

HEBREWS 1:9

Man of Joy

What is your personal portrait of Christ? Do you visualize him walking through crowds and towns with an austere or somber countenance? Do you see him speaking with the disciples late at night in stern tones?

Well, Jesus certainly accomplished the most serious work of humankind—reconciling sinful people with a holy God. And he no doubt spent a good deal of his time on earth in devout contemplation. He was, after all, a "man of sorrows, and familiar with suffering" (Isaiah 53:3).

But the anguish and pain the Savior felt because of our sins did not diminish his unexcelled joy. Jesus, the God-Man, was and is a thoroughly joyous person.

Can you image Christ never laughing or smiling as he went about his trade of carpentry for almost thirty years? Do you not think he enjoyed some lively exchanges of conversation with his customers? Who wants to do business with a stern carpenter?

Can you picture Jesus at the wedding at Cana sitting in a corner, isolated and detached from the festivities? When Jesus called men to follow him as his disciples, do you suppose that men would walk away from their livelihood for a joyless Messiah?

Jesus was deadly serious about his mission of redemption. The Scriptures are clear about that. But they also let us know that the Savior, while on the road to the cross, had a profound possession of true joy in the Father. Christ could bear the grievous sins of man at Calvary because of the "joy set before him" (Hebrews 12:2).

As you live in personal fellowship with Christ today, you are engaged in relationship with the source of all joy. When you come before him in prayer and entreaty, you come to the High Priest, who delights in hearing and answering your petitions. The angels in heaven rejoice when sinners come to Christ, because they have entered into eternal joy.

We could never ask for the gift of joy if the Giver was joyless. Heaven would not be our supreme delight if sheer joy did not permeate our eternal existence. Christ is the one in whom we can delight, because he is the most delightful and winsome person in heaven or earth. John Piper writes that "we are converted when Christ becomes for us a Treasure Chest of holy joy."

As you read the Scriptures and come to Christ in prayer, remember you come to the one who came to give us "a crown of beauty instead of ashes, the oil of gladness instead of mourning" (Isaiah 61:3).

———— ❖ ————

Jesus, you are the man of joy, and you live joyously in my heart. You are the supreme giver of joy, because no one else is as purely joyful as you. Let me come to you each day as my divine source of delight. Thank you for dying for our sins and for the joy set before us.

Touchstone

Jesus is a joyous person

who delights in sharing

his happiness with us.

Give thanks to the LORD, for he is good.

PSALM 136:1

Many Thanks

artha Washington wrote that happiness is more a matter of "disposition" than a result of our circumstances. Several hundred years have passed since the wife of President George Washington made that observation, but her insight remains as applicable today as it was then.

Disposition is, quite simply, our prevailing attitude. There are people who live in circumstances that others envy, but whose attitude about themselves, others, and their lot in life is consistently disagreeable. They are an unhappy bunch whose acquaintance few care to make. Conversely, there are people whose circumstances give them good reason to complain, but their attitude is surprisingly cheerful, their demeanor uncommonly pleasant.

I remember one particular morning many years ago when I was discouraged. I just woke up that way. I spent some time in God's Word, but my mood did not change. I decided to go to work, even though it was extremely early. Along the way, I went to a small drive-thru and ordered a biscuit. The elderly man who greeted me at the drive-thru window was amazingly cheerful. We talked for a minute while the order was filled, and as he handed me my food, I asked him why he was so merry in the wee hours of the morning. "Well, I don't take any day for granted at my age, and I have made it a habit to thank God for the gift of another day." I drove away encouraged, and I have never forgotten his bright words.

A thankful person is a joyful person. The person who learns to keep a grateful heart in spite of everything has the best opportunity to maintain a joyful outlook on life. When we are genuinely thankful to the Lord for his blessings, the chances are excellent that our disposition will be pleasing to the Lord and to those around us.

The best place to start for a thankful attitude is to simply do it. "Give thanks in all circumstances, for this is God's will for you in Christ Jesus" (1 Thessalonians 5:18). We don't have to understand all the implications, we just need to start obeying the Lord's instructions.

Can you think of some things to thank God for? If your attitude has gone sour, it may take a few minutes to come up with a list, but you can usually find something. Perhaps your problems have been so overwhelming that thanksgiving seems inappropriate, almost insincere. God understands your emotions, but if you learn to thank him, though your circumstances may not change, your attitude will. You can thank him that he loves you, has given his Son for your sins, sympathizes with your weaknesses, promises to meet every need, is generous in every respect, faithful in all situations—you get the idea. God wants and deserves our gratitude, and the more we thank him, the more our attitude is positively affected.

Let me ask you this question: "What do you have to lose by giving thanks to God?" I challenge you to spend some concentrated time just giving thanks to the Lord. Take a long time-out from complaining. At the end of the day, see if your attitude isn't changed for the better. Do it consistently, and your obedience can pour the footings for a life grounded in the joy of the Lord.

I realized the only thing I have to lose, Father, if I am thankful is a less than Spirit-filled attitude. I choose to praise you now for your overwhelming generosity to me. I give thanks to you for the very thing that has adversely affected my thinking and living. Keep my heart focused on you, not the problem.

Touchstone

We can't be joyful if
we're not thankful.

Though now for a little while you may have had to suffer grief in all kinds of trials.

1 PETER 1:6

No Surprise

When trouble blows in and stays for a while, our joy seems to fade to the fringes of our existence. Our reservoir of joy is drained by the stress and strain, and even a smile is hard to come by. How can we possibly entertain joy when hardship is our uninvited house guest?

Here is the paradoxical, but absolutely critical truth: Trouble is not the enemy of joy, but its friend. "Consider it pure joy, my brothers, whenever you face trials of many kinds" (James 1:2). Is that abnormal or what? Humanly speaking, it certainly is. But from God's perspective, the viewpoint of ultimate reality, the grinding seasons of life can actually stimulate our experience of joy, not crush it.

Here is God's perspective: "Consider it pure joy, my brothers, whenever you face trials of many kinds, because you know that the testing of your faith develops perseverance. Perseverance must finish its work so that you may be mature and complete, not lacking anything" (James 1:2–4).

Consider it pure joy. The Greek word translated "consider" incorporates accounting terminology. It means to "reckon" or "calculate." This helps. Trials don't make us feel joyful. That's nonsense. But we can take a look at our problems and mark it down as a fact that our trials can add up to joy if we respond to them correctly.

How is this possible? *Knowing that the testing of your faith develops perseverance.* Our disappointments and difficulties have a specific role—they test our faith. Will we cling to God in our adversity or turn to some other source of comfort? Will we continue trusting the Lord to help us or turn away from him? Faith is indispensable in the life of the believer. It's what we live by.

When our faith comes under the gun and we continue to keep our eyes on Christ, spiritual muscle is being formed. Hardship, when endured with dependence on Christ, actually serves to strengthen us. *Perseverance must finish its work, so that you may be mature and complete, not lacking in anything.* Our ability to go the distance is enhanced. We gain power for the rough journey ahead. We're better prepared to handle the next battle. Our trials make us seasoned veterans of faith, men and women of integrity who have been through the heat of spiritual struggle and have retained our confidence in the Lord. The strain becomes strength.

Don't allow trials to destroy your joy. You may have no sensation of cheer as you deal with your heartaches, but God's joy is on the rise when you least expect it. Faith is being mustered, endurance is acquired, and spiritual maturity is being developed. The joy is not in the process, but in the outcome. God is once again working all things together for good.

And to our surprise, but not God's, our tribulations are paving the way for growing joy.

I have not welcomed my trials as friends, Lord, because I haven't seen my troubles from your perspective. But I do understand now through the Scripture that they can bring me close to you and steel my faith. I don't like the problems I'm dealing with now, but I will, with your help, allow them to press me close to your presence. I thank you that nothing can separate me from your love.

Touchstone

A tested faith is a sure
foundation for strong joy.

Miserable comforters are you all!

Not So Joyful

---⊛---

The writer of Ecclesiastes said there was a time for everything, including a "time to weep and a time to laugh, a time to mourn and a time to dance" (Ecclesiastes 3:4). Expressive joy is not always appropriate. When the occasion is somber, we do well to remember that you don't "sing songs to a heavy heart" (Proverbs 25:20).

The Scriptures advise us to "rejoice with those who rejoice; mourn with those who mourn" (Romans 12:15). When a person is grieving, don't indulge in spiritual platitudes that offer little or no solace at the time. Instead, put your arm around them, be available when you're needed, and cry with them. The Lord will help them with their ache and heart; you hand them a handkerchief, bring them a meal, or send them a card. They need compassion, a listening ear, a sympathetic heart, not a sermon. When Jesus came to Mary and Martha's house after Lazarus' death, he heard the loud wails, saw the anguish, and "wept."

We should also know that times of personal tribulations are never pleasant, especially when God is working to dislodge and remove areas of deep-rooted, but grievous, belief and behavior. "No discipline seems pleasant at the time, but painful" (Hebrews 12:11). When God is dealing with us, we don't welcome the pain. The struggle and the upheaval that accompany God's corrective hand sting badly. It is only "later on" (v. 11) that we can look back and see God's good hand in it all.

It is also important to remember that sorrow is spiritually legitimate. Again Solomon counsels that "sorrow is better than laughter, because a sad face is good for the heart" (Ecclesiastes 7:3).

We learn much about ourselves and about God in seasons of sadness. We pass through baleful valleys so that we might one day be a comfort to others traveling the same road (2 Corinthians 1:3–5). Robert Browning Hamilton wrote:

> I walked with Sorrow
> And not a word said she;
> But oh, the things I learned from her
> when Sorrow walked with me.

The apostle Paul's pointed letter to the church in Corinth troubled and vexed many of the readers. Yet their sorrow led them to godly repentance so that Paul could say, "You became sorrowful as God intended" (2 Corinthians 7:9). Sin, as it should, brought sorrow, and God used it as always for his good purposes.

In God's ever mysterious paradox, sorrow and joy coexist. Since our joy is not founded on circumstance or emotion, it still runs deep, even in our moments of deep distress. We should allow sorrow to do its painful but necessary work in our lives with our faith still firmly anchored in Christ's rich joy.

And always remember that though "weeping may remain for a night," we can know that "rejoicing comes in the morning" (Psalm 30:5).

———— • ————

There have been times of sadness and sorrow in my life, Father. I am so grateful that you understand these seasons and use them to accentuate your participating presence in my life. Nothing is wasted in my walk with you, and no tear is unnoticed. I need never be overwhelmed by any grief or heartache since your joy abides deep in my spirit through your presence.

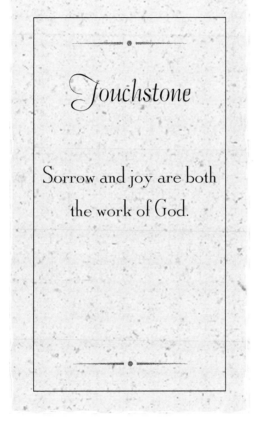

Touchstone

Sorrow and joy are both
the work of God.

Encourage the timid, help the weak, be patient with everyone.

1 THESSALONIANS 5:14

Pass It Around

The apostle Paul's letter to the Philippian church from the confines of a prison is remarkably upbeat. Although Paul mentions his internment as he begins his epistle, he never allows his chains to dictate his attitude.

Paul's reason for joy, other than his intensely personal fellowship with the Savior, is the relationship he developed with the believers in Philippi: "In all my prayers for all of you, I always pray with joy because of your partnership in the gospel" (Philippians 1:4–5). Despite the miserable conditions he was in and the distinct possibility of death, Paul knew his work with the church wasn't finished. "I know that I will remain, and I will continue with all of you for your progress and joy in the faith" (v. 25).

Throughout his ministry, Paul found much of his joy linked to the well-being of those he served (2 Corinthians 1:24; 1 Thessalonians 2:19–20; Philemon 1:7). Paul's troubles and aggravations were mitigated by the knowledge that his life in Christ had been a blessing and encouragement to others.

Especially as we mature in the faith, we learn to find more of our fulfillment in the happiness of others. Few things in life bring me more pleasure than my grandchildren. I find great satisfaction in knowing that neighbors, friends, and family are growing strong in the Lord. I am thrilled when I hear how God has answered the prayers of a friend. I get excited when I see others find truth in the Scriptures that transforms their behavior and thoughts.

Seeking ways to help others find joy in Christ is a practical means of putting the interests of others above our own and is a decidedly Christlike mind-set (Philippians 2:3). It indicates that we have made solid progress in our Christian life, not merely focusing on the vanity of self-gratification that so often preoccupies our thoughts and endeavors.

Actually, when we make it a priority to see God's joy active in others, something amazing begins to happen—we see our own joy increase. Nothing made Paul happier than to see those he taught become solid citizens of the faith. The more we delight in the cheer of others, the more our souls are supernaturally replenished. Almost imperceptibly, we discover renewed vitality. We have forgotten about ourselves for a while, and we are clearly the better off because of it.

If you're looking for joy, don't look in all the wrong places. It can be in the recovery of a sick friend whom you've visited or the encouragement of a dispirited church member you invited to lunch. There are countless ways and days to spend in seeking the joy of others.

Seldom will you be disappointed.

---- ● ----

There are so many people who need to know your joy and peace, Lord. Lead me to those with whom I can share your love in practical and meaningful ways. Help me to start with those closest to me, to serve them with a new attitude. Keep me from pride and love of ease that prevent your joy from flowing through my life to others.

Touchstone

Joy multiplies when you

spread it around.

Everlasting joy will be theirs.

ISAIAH 61:7

Sheer Joy

———— ◉ ————

The Holy Spirit had just been poured out on the fledgling New Testament church. Banding together, the small but growing group of Christians were known not only for their love but for their unfettered joy. "They were taking their meals together with gladness and sincerity of heart, praising God and having favor with all the people" (Acts 2:46–47 NASB).

One early church writer commented that "joy was the distinctive hallmark of the Christian." With the promise of both abundant and eternal life, Christians have every right to be the keepers of transcendent joy.

In Jesus' Sermon on the Mount, he explained that those who lived by the principles of his kingdom would be "blessed"— literally, "happy, fortunate, to be envied."

David danced before the Lord. When he sinned before the Lord by committing adultery with Bathsheba, one telling sign of his estrangement before Jehovah was a dearth of joy—"Restore to me the joy of your salvation" (Psalm 51:12).

The Hebrews of the Old Testament had numerous feasts that were characterized by corporate glee and thanksgiving. When the returning Jewish captives from the Babylonian exile began the construction of the temple, they "shouted aloud for joy" (Ezra 3:12 NASB).

Throughout Scripture, men and women of faith are presented as people of joy. Their trials, battles, and stern encounters with life's adversities served only to lead them deeper into the glad heart of God.

Our testimony before an all too joyless world, incessantly seeking but never finding enduring happiness, should be characterized by extraordinary, palpable joy.

Do our words convey the wonder of our intimate relationship with a loving Savior? Do our faces tell of the inner peace and security we have in Christ? Does our demeanor speak of the presence of the one who was anointed with the oil of gladness?

Those who live without Christ in this world have no transcendent meaning for their existence and thus no real basis for joy. Those who belong to Christ, who revel in the pleasures of fatherly love, have every reason to exult. Our home in heaven is secure; Christ's provision for our needs on earth is certain.

When Christ returns for his church—his people—and establishes his kingdom, the joy and glory of God will fill the earth. Sorrow and sadness will not exist; the gloriously happy God will reign forever with his holy joy.

———— ◆ ————

What a wonderful, awesome God you are. You are the sole source of true, enduring joy, and it is your gift to me through faith in your Son, Christ. Fill me with increasing joy as I delight myself in you and learn daily of you. I thank you, because in your paths, there is fullness of joy.

Touchstone

Great joy comes from

a great God.

The thief comes only to steal and kill and destroy; I have come that they may have life, and have it to the full.

JOHN 10:10

Spoiling the Thief

Jesus came to save us from our sins so that we might experience life at its best. This is what Jesus told his audience in his discourse in the tenth chapter of John. As the Good Shepherd, Christ takes care of his flock, protects us, and leads us into an abundant life.

Since this is the case, why then do we so often lack joy? Why are so many days lackluster? Obviously, there are some painful trials and nagging problems that can be the culprit, but I think we need to be clear on one major issue: Satan, the enemy of our soul, likes nothing better than to see Christians live joylessly.

Although Jesus' analogous reference to the "thief" depicts the selfish interests of false religious leaders of Israel's past, the notion that Satan can and does attempt to steal our zest for Christ is clearly biblical. Satan is called a "murderer" and malicious "liar" who can no longer threaten our eternal security in Christ, but can wreak havoc with our temporal state of affairs. If he can persistently snatch away our joy, our testimony is dampened and our spiritual disciplines eroded.

We are in grave danger if we do not acknowledge and recognize that we are in a spiritual battle. The life in Christ we have entered into by faith is a supernatural one with an evil archenemy who is bent on making our life miserable. When we find ourselves going through days with spirits that are downcast and dull, we must remember that the evil one is craftily behind the scenes at work.

C. S. Lewis writes in *The Screwtape Letters* of Satan's dark schemes to attack believers caught in the "trough of dulness or 'dryness.'" The senior devil Screwtape, conversing with a junior devil, Wormwood, describes his tactics: "In the first place I have always found the Trough periods of the human undulation provide excellent opportunity for all sensual temptations. . . . The attack has a much better chance of success when the man's whole inner world is drab and cold and empty."

The illicit but potent tactic of tainting our joy is one of the most powerful tools in his dark arsenal. We need not be afraid of Satan or his schemes as we learn about God's truth, but we must not underestimate his activity in adversely affecting our minds and hearts.

What I have found to be most effective against the devil's ploys to deprive us of our rightful joy in the Lord is this: Praise Christ for his victory over sin, Satan, and all evil. Praise declares the greatness and goodness of the Lord and allows us to enter his presence with the right frame of mind. It affirms his unceasing activity in our life and clears the spirit of doubt and confusion.

I have found that praising God for his triumph over my foe is a powerful, biblical way to regain my enjoyment of Christ and his provision for me. God routed Satan at the cross (Colossians 2:15), and when we thank him for his conquest of the Evil One at Calvary, we remind Satan that he is a bloodied and defeated enemy. All of the joy we need is ours in Christ, and Satan will not succeed in his plot to diminish it.

Praising God for his victory works because it is spiritual truth put into action. The devil will try and try again to steal our joy, but he cannot as long as we stand on the solid ground of Christ's triumph over him.

———— ◆ ————

I take great comfort in knowing that you have conquered the enemy of my soul. Help me to daily acknowledge your victorious presence in my life and to experience the reality of the overcoming life that is mine in Jesus Christ.

Touchstone

Praise is the powerful
ally of joy.

Yet not as I will, but as you will.

The Way of Submission

---- ✦ ----

God's ways are not our ways, said the prophet Isaiah, and that spiritual axiom is probably never more true than when it concerns the relationship between joy and submission.

Our perspective on submission is pretty straightforward—we like to be submitted to rather than to submit to another. We want to be first, not second, or third. We prefer the role of master, not servant. Submission has a clear and certain stigma we want to avoid.

Jesus, of course, turns all that rationalization on its head. The Lord of all became the Servant of all, kneeling at his disciple's feet with towel in hand. He lived in perfect submission to the Father, subordinating his will to the Father's plan and purpose. But in surrender, he gained everything, including joy for eternity by becoming the Savior of the world.

Submission, as practiced by Christ and modeled for us, is always to the will of the Father. Though Jesus came to die on the cross for our sins, he approached the event that would separate him from the Father with intense emotion. "My Father, if it is possible, may this cup be taken from me. Yet not as I will, but as you will" (Matthew 26:39). Surrender is always to the will of the Father. We think we know the answer, but it isn't working. We believe we can solve the problem, but it doesn't go away. The only way through the predicament is humbly bowing to the will of God, saying, "Lord, I give up on making this work. Despite all I have done, I do not have your peace or joy. I am unable to resolve this problem. I surrender to your will and ask that you work your will in this situation." At that moment, God's supernatural wisdom and power are put into motion. Our strong and stubborn wills have submitted to the Father's desire and plan.

F. B. Meyer, the great preacher, said: "It is in proportion as we see God's will in the various events of life and surrender ourselves either to bear it or do it, that we shall find earth's bitter circumstances becoming sweet and its hard things easy."

What bitter thing are you facing now? What hard thing are you dealing with that just won't go away? Fighting against our pain, trying harder to do the right thing, as admirable as our motives may be, simply won't work if we haven't come to the place of surrender.

Surrender is not quitting or giving up, it is giving in to Christ. Surrender is not passive resignation; it is relinquishing our rights to the Lord and asking him to do things his way.

Meyer tells us that God has placed us in our current circumstances "by [his] appointment, in his keeping, under his tutelage, for his time."

God has a plan. Submit your will to his and enter into the joy of seeing God work in marvelous and wonderful ways.

———— ◆ ————

Create a submissive and yielded spirit in me. I'm not sure what your plans or purposes are in this circumstance, but I can trust you. Help me to let go of my agenda, my preconceived notions as to how this problem should be resolved, and relinquish the settlement to you. You are able.

Touchstone

The Lord of all became
the Servant of all.

For the kingdom of God is … righteousness, peace and joy in the Holy Spirit.

ROMANS 14:17

The Joy of the Lord

———— ❖ ————

Nehemiah coined the phrase "the joy of the LORD" as the Hebrews heard the Word of God afresh after many years of neglecting God's instructions. The throng wept as they heard the great truths of Scripture, and Nehemiah encouraged the people not to grieve any longer, "for the joy of the LORD is your strength" (Nehemiah 8:10).

The principle remains in force: God's joy gives us the stamina we need to deal with obstacles and opposition. There are appropriate seasons for grief and sorrow, but to nurture them courts lethargy and melancholy. God's joy fuels our confidence, strengthens our spiritual fiber, and gives us hope for the future.

But what is the joy of the Lord? How can we experience it?

The joy of the Lord is independent of circumstances. Whenever our joy is connected to the conditions of our environment, we are destined for wild fluctuations. This won't work because there are too many periods of adversity, too many bouts with frustrating problems. Joy will ride on the winds of favorable or unfavorable happenings. We make the errant choice of looking for our joy in all the wrong places. What seems secure today can vanish tomorrow. What appears to be the rational choice now can bring great disappointment later.

The joy of the Lord is independent of feelings. Like circumstances, our emotions are unreliable. Some mornings we awaken with a great sense of well-being. On other days, we rise with feelings of dread or anxiety. None of our feelings are to be trusted, nor are they capable of sustaining the joy of the Lord.

The joy of the Lord is dependent on our faith in an unchanging Lord, in his plans and purposes for our lives. So wise and good is God's plan for us that John Newton wrote: "If it were possible for me to alter any part of his plan, I could only spoil it." Faith in God's gracious provision is the ignition key to experiencing God's joy. "May the God of hope fill you with all joy and peace as you trust in him" (Romans 15:13).

The joy of the Lord is accompanied with two familiar companions—peace and hope. When God's joy is ours, so are his peace and hope. The problems may be perplexing, but the peace that transcends circumstances keeps our minds steady on God. The outlook may be inauspicious, but our hope is grounded on the unfailing love of God. Wherever God's joy is abundant, his peace prevails and our hope is firmly anchored.

The joy of the Lord is a gift from God. "Every good and perfect gift is from above, coming down from the Father of the heavenly lights, who does not change like shifting shadows" (James 1:17). The joy of the Lord flows from heaven down, and our responsibility is to simply receive it and enjoy it by faith.

I am so thankful that your joy is unceasingly fresh and alive. My strength comes from banking on your inexhaustible supply of gladness and hope, in the good times and the bad. Your plans are for my welfare and my good, to give me a future and hope.

Touchstone

God's joy fuels our faith
to face future obstacles.

All my fountains are in you.

PSALM 87:7

The Source of Joy

---●---

*I*n C. S. Lewis's classic work of fiction, *The Silver Chair*, a lost and thirsty girl comes upon a brook guarded by the lion Aslan. Frightened by the lion, symbolic of Christ, Jill nonetheless engages him in conversation.

"Are you thirsty?" said the Lion.

"I'm dying of thirst," said Jill.

"Then drink," said the Lion.

"May I—could I—would you mind going away while I do?" said Jill.

The lion answered this only by a look and a very low growl. And as Jill gazed at its motionless bulk, she realized that she might as well have asked the whole mountain to move aside for her convenience.

The delicious rippling noise of the stream was driving her nearly frantic.

"Will you promise not to do—do anything to me, if I do come?" said Jill.

"I will make no promise," said the Lion.

Jill was so thirsty now that, without noticing it, she had come a step nearer.

"Do you eat girls?" she said.

"I have swallowed up girls and boys, women and men, kings and emperors, cities and realms," said the Lion. It didn't say this as if it were boasting, nor as if it were sorry, nor as if it were angry. It just said it.

"I daren't come and drink," said Jill.

"Then you will die of thirst," said the Lion.

"Oh dear!" said Jill, coming another step nearer. "I suppose I must go and look for another stream then."

"There is no other stream," said the Lion.

Our thirst for significance can be satisfied only in the person of Christ. He is the source of all joy. All the pleasures we seek in people or things will not quench our parched souls. God lets us drink from his "river of delights" (Psalm 36:8) and turns our emotional deserts into streams (Psalm 107:35).

Are you afraid he might ask you to let go of something or someone you hold dear? Are you worried you might not find all you are searching for in him? Lay aside your fears, look nowhere else for fulfillment, and come to him. He will not disappoint you. He will bless you more than you can possibly imagine. He will grace your life with depths of joy you have never experienced.

When Jill overcame her unfounded fears of Aslan and stooped to drink, "it was the coldest, most refreshing water she had ever tasted. You didn't need to drink much of it, because it quenched your thirst at once."

Christ invites you to let him satisfy your deepest longings for joy. "Come, all you who are thirsty, come to the waters.... Listen, listen to me ... and your soul will delight in the richest of fare" (Isaiah 51–2).

Lord, I come to drink from the fountain of your delights today. I know that when I bring my needs, burdens, hopes, and fears to you, you refresh, encourage, and uplift my spirit. I realize that nothing can satisfy my longings except you. Turn my deserts into streams of living water with the knowledge of your loving presence and power.

Touchstone

Christ alone satisfies our
deepest longings.

Then you will know the truth, and the truth will set you free.

JOHN 8:32

Truth or Feelings

⸻ ⚙ ⸻

*O*ur feelings play a dominant role in our attitude and aptitude. On agreeable days when all seems well with our soul and our circumstances, our emotions can produce a degree of euphoria. We tackle problems with greater energy and creativity and handle adversity with more confidence.

The Lord certainly isn't averse to our emotional and mental well-being (2 John 1:2), but it is a mistake to base our joy on our feelings. If we are cheerful and competent only when favorable winds blow, then our concept and experience of Christ's joy is fatally flawed.

This is because there are days when we feel good and days when we feel bad. When the disagreeable days come, and they *do* come, how will we handle them? Will we be grouchy, impatient, angry, perturbed, or exasperated? If we rely on the fluctuating barometer of emotions, the answer is ordinarily a decided yes.

The great news of the gospel is that the truth will always set us free. The truth of God is none other than his Word. The Scripture is God's baseline for all truth, and the more we know his truth, the more freedom we have to live joyfully apart from our finicky feelings.

Here are a few emotions that cause our joy to fade along with the corresponding truth that builds our well-being on the infallible ground of God's tested and proven truth.

> Feeling: I am unworthy or unacceptable in God's eyes.
> Truth: I am accepted and worthy in Christ (Psalm 139;
>   Romans 15:7).
>
> Feeling: I am cannot solve the problems I face.

Truth: I have God's wisdom for all situations (James 1:5).

Feeling: I am unloved.

Truth: God loves me (John 15:9; Romans 8:35–39).

Feeling: I am too weak to make it through the day.

Truth: I have all the strength I need in Christ (Psalms 37:34; Philippians 4:19).

Feeling: I am depressed and hopeless.

Truth: I have all the hope I need through Christ (Psalm 16:11; Romans 15:13).

Feeling: I can't change anything about me or my circumstances.

Truth: God's power is greater than any habit or problem and is at work in me to bring about positive change (Ephesians 3:20).

God's incredibly rich joy is never coupled to our changing passions or feelings. It is founded on the constant truth of his Word. To experience this kind of joy, we must cultivate the habit of regular meditation on the great truths of Scripture.

They are the only foundation for the kind of joy that will sustain us when our feelings drag us into the mire of muddled thinking and negatively charged emotions. The truth sets us and keeps us free.

———— ◆ ————

I come to learn more of you, Lord. Your truth can set me free from negative, crippling emotions. You came to set the captives free, and I confess that I have been a slave to flawed, false thinking.

I am tired of this kind of bondage and look to you, Jesus, to transform me through your powerful truth.

Touchstone

The truth sets us
and keep us free.

Let us not become weary in doing good, for at the proper
time we will reap a harvest if we do not give up.

GALATIANS 6:9

When You're Weary

──────────── ❖ ────────────

Vince Lombardi was a legendary coach with the Green Bay Packers. He built a football dynasty based on the physical toughness of his players and an indomitable spirit. Yet one of his most oft repeated comments is one we all can relate to: "Fatigue," Lombardi remarked, "makes cowards of us all."

That's a truism that the prophet Elijah would certainly endorse. Fresh from a dominating clash with false prophets that saw Elijah call fire down from heaven, Elijah found himself on the run from an evil queen. The Lord recognized the root of Elijah's sudden cravenness and prescribed a pretty simple remedy—food and rest.

Elijah was whipped. He was tired in body, mind, and soul. Few conditions deplete our joy more rapidly and completely than weariness. When we are tired, the sense of God's joy is virtually nil.

Thankfully, the Lord understands our frail frames and doesn't engage in pointless condemnation or futile lectures in self-improvement. Rather, he gently leads us to some rejuvenating spiritual principles that can restore our souls.

Sometimes, we need to follow Elijah's tactics. Take a step back from the situation and let the Lord refresh us. We may need a physical break like a day off from work or a day away from the kids. A change of scenery for a short time can help clear our minds and give us some perspective on the circumstances. Or we may need to simply bring our burdens to the Lord and rest in him. This means we trust him with increasing confidence that he is willing and able to come to our aid with the wisdom and power that we lack. "Come to me, all you who are weary and burdened, and I will give you rest," Jesus said (Matthew 11:28). Coming to Christ in faith can transform our exhaustion into newfound energy.

At other times, we need to be patient and realize that God promises that we will "reap" and be "rewarded" in due time. Much of our weariness stems from a common ailment of wanting to see our problems resolved *now*. That's the way we like it, but it isn't the way God works. Reaping follows sowing. We may be bone tired of trying, but if we don't quit, an answer will come. Our "labor in the Lord is not in vain" (1 Corinthians 15:58), meaning that God will reward our efforts in his timing.

The farmer who plants his crops works through his pain and tiredness by looking forward to the fruit of his labor (James 5:7). The joy is subdued for a season, but it runs over at an appropriate time. Our joy can survive throughout the demanding seasons of life. Learn when to take a time-out, drawing new strength from him, and when to keep on plodding, knowing that God has great things in store, if we remain faithful.

I get so tired sometimes that I don't think I can take another step or face another day. Help me, Father, to turn to you for the strength I need and give me wisdom to know when I need a physical break. You were tired and weary yourself, Jesus, so you know how I feel.

Touchstone

God invites the weary
and the weak to come to
him for refreshment.

Be filled with the Spirit.

EPHESIANS 5:18

Winning the Battle for Joy

here is a gigantic tug of war pushing and pulling within the life of the believer for the reign of joy. The apostle Paul describes the contest this way: "For the sinful nature desires what is contrary to the Spirit, and the Spirit what is contrary to the sinful nature. They are in conflict with each other" (Galatians 5:17). Consistently experiencing the joy of the Lord is both hard and easy: hard, because our flesh is bent toward strife and striving; easy, because the Spirit of God provides all the joy we need.

The sinful nature, or our human instincts and behavior apart from the Holy Spirit's influence, constantly seeks to drag us into the morass of selfish living. The Holy Spirit, whom we received in his fullness at salvation, imparts the kind of joy that transcends our circumstances and transforms our hearts. The joy of the Spirit is the only joy that works in the trenches of reality.

We move into experiencing the joy of the Spirit by first knowing that it is already ours, not something we must earnestly attain. We have been given the Spirit. He resides in our soul, deposited as the guarantee of God's presence and future provision (Ephesians 1:13–14). There are no special ceremonies, no rote steps, no amount of personal determination that will secure the joy of the Holy Spirit in your life. You possess it now through the Spirit.

This incredible joy—joy that is undiminished by circumstances—grows steadily in our hearts as we abide in Christ. Jesus talked about the vine and branches in the fifteenth chapter of John, describing the source of all vitality in the Christian life. "I am the vine; you are the branches. If a man remains in me and I in him, he will bear much fruit" (John 15:5). Joy is the fruit, the product, of a life ruled by the Spirit. The word picture is vivid; the joy we all want comes by living in union with Christ through the Spirit. Take a look at an apple orchard. The branches hang low with apples because they take their nourishment and appearance from the life of the tree. We bear the trademarks of a joyful Christian life as we draw from the source of all joy—the person of Christ who indwells us through the Spirit.

The key to abiding is daily yielding to the gracious influence of the Holy Spirit. It is submitting our inclinations, our protests, and our agendas to the Lord and asking the Spirit of God to saturate our minds and steer our actions. It is obeying the truth we know, refusing to end the day with anger in our hearts, forgiving those who have hurt us, repenting of the sins that have throttled us.

As we do, the Holy Spirit overcomes the dismal works of the flesh, our vain and futile attempts to find lasting joy apart from life in Christ. We can't overcome the flesh—that is the work of the Spirit who daily offers us his conquering character.

Joy can be ours, for the Spirit of God gives it freely and lavishly to those who abide daily in him.

———— ❖ ————

Lord, trusting in my own strength has only resulted in spiritual defeat and disappointment. You sent the Holy Spirit to enable us to experience victory and joy over the enemy. It is in his power I choose to face each battle every day with confidence and joy that I will be victorious.

Touchstone

Only the Holy Spirit can produce the fruit of the Spirit.

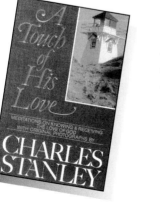

A Touch of His Freedom:
Meditations on Freedom
in Christ
Hardcover 0-310-54620-6

A Touch of His Goodness:
Meditations on God's
Abundant Goodness
Hardcover 0-310-21489-0

A Touch of His Love:
Meditations on Knowing and
Receiving the Love of God
Hardcover 0-310-54560-9

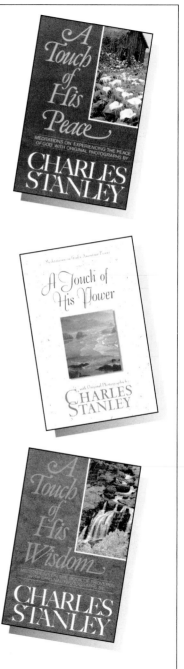

The Blessings of Brokenness:
Why God Allows Us to Go Through Hard Times

No matter how great your faith in God, pain and grief are a part of life.

Perhaps you've already experienced circumstances so shattering you may wonder today whether it's even possible to pick up the pieces. And maybe you can't. But God can—and the good news is, he wants to reassemble the shards of your life into a wholeness that only the broken can know.

With gentle wisdom, Dr. Stanley shines light on the process of being broken. He reveals the ways we protest against it. And he gives us an inspiring look beyond the pain to the promise of blessing.

Hardcover 0-310-20026-1
Audio Pages® Abridged Cassettes
0-310-20421-6

GRAND RAPIDS, MICHIGAN 49530

www.zondervan.com

We want to hear from you. Please send your comments about this book to us in care of the address below. Thank you.

ZONDERVAN™

GRAND RAPIDS, MICHIGAN 49530

www.zondervan.com